Sweeter than Honey

52-week devotional journal for women

Belle City Gifts
Savage, Minnesota, USA
Belle City Gifts is an imprint of BroadStreet Publishing Group, LLC.
Broadstreetpublishing.com

Sweeter than Honey

9781424570409

Typesetting and design by Garborg Design Works | garborgdesign.com
Compiled and edited by Michelle Winger | literallyprecise.com

Printed in China.

25 26 27 28 29 30 31 7 6 5 4 3 2 1

How sweet your
words taste to me;
they are sweeter than honey.
Your commandments give
me understanding.
PSALM 119:103-104 NLT

Introduction

The immediate reward of honey is its sweet taste. But honey also has incredible health benefits. Similarly, God's Word has both instant and lasting advantages. The wisdom found within its pages requires time spent searching and meditating. True understanding happens through prayer and an intimate relationship with God.

Be encouraged as you savor the Scriptures and meditations in this weekly devotional journal. Ponder thought-provoking questions and write your reflections in the spaces provided.

God has shown immeasurable love and grace, and his undeserved kindness is revealed in his mercies that are new every morning. Taste the goodness of his lifegiving words that are both sweet and strong and be nourished by the richness of his wisdom and compassion.

Reflect on the promises of God, delight in his goodness, and express your thoughts, prayers, and praise in the space provided.

WEEK 1

Sustenance

Sustain me, my God, according to your promise,
and I will live;
do not let my hopes be dashed.

PSALM 119:116 NIV

What keeps you going throughout your day? Could it be a midday nap, an afternoon cup of tea, or a walk that gets the blood flowing? Whatever the method of choice, all of us have things that help sustain us through our long days. Beyond the midday slump, our souls require sustaining, too, and whether we realize it or not, we are constantly on the search for something that will fill us, satisfy our hunger, and give us a reason to wake up and go day after day.

God promises to sustain you; he brings life and hope where other things fall short. Take account of the state of your heart in this moment. What are you giving yourself to in hope of satisfaction? What are you pursuing in anticipation of numbing your pain? It is in Christ alone that your hope will not be dashed. Set aside all else and find your peace in him.

Reflection

What things have you pursued that only give energy for a short period of time? Were you disappointed when that ran out? How can you seek God instead of drifting toward that false support the next time you are in need?

MY THOUGHTS

After reflecting on this devotion and follow-up questions, here are my thoughts.

MY RESPONSE

This is how I can apply the message to my life.

This hope will not disappoint us, because God's love has been poured out into our hearts through the Holy Spirit who was given to us.

ROMANS 5:5 CSB

To me, this Scripture feels most like (check one)

☐ A PROMISE ☐ AN INSTRUCTION ☐ A TRUTH

Here's how it impacts me…

....

....

....

....

....

Prayer

GRATITUDE

I have been blessed with so many good things.
Here is what I am particularly thankful for this week.

REQUESTS

After reading and reflecting, here is what I'm asking God for.

WEEK 2

Beautiful Inheritance

> The Lord is my chosen portion and my cup;
> you hold my lot.
> The lines have fallen for me in pleasant places;
> indeed, I have a beautiful inheritance.
>
> PSALM 16:5-6 ESV

Perhaps you woke up this morning considering all the things that are not right in your life: your finances, your marriage, your job, your health. There are countless things in life that can be put in the category of "grievances," but today is a day for recognizing God's goodness.

Regardless of your circumstances today, you have been chosen by God to be a part of his family, and therefore you are blessed. Whether you have good health or not, whether your relationships are happy ones or not, your joy is not dependent on those things. You have a beautiful inheritance in Christ, and while the culmination of God's blessings has not yet arrived, the realization of his goodness starts today. Will you, like the wandering Israelites, demand relief from pain and insecurity, or will you choose Christ as your portion, the source of all you will ever need?

Reflection

Consider the many ways you have been blessed. You have the hope of a beautiful inheritance. How can this cause your heart to rest in contentment today?

MY THOUGHTS

After reflecting on this devotion and follow-up questions, here are my thoughts.

MY RESPONSE

This is how I can apply the message to my life.

You are my portion, Lord;
I have promised to obey
your words

PSALM 119:57 NIV

To me, this Scripture feels most like (check one)

☐ A PROMISE ☐ AN INSTRUCTION ☐ A TRUTH

Here's how it impacts me...

PRAYER

GRATITUDE

I have been blessed with so many good things.
Here is what I am particularly thankful for this week.

REQUESTS

After reading and reflecting, here is what I'm asking God for.

WEEK 3

Truly Good

> You are good and do only good;
> teach me your decrees.
>
> PSALM 119:68 NLT

Who among us would knowingly let ourselves be led by false teachers or deceivers claiming to have our best interests in mind? Every day we are up against the deceptions of this world, and many times we allow ourselves to be misled by that which looks good but actually plots to destroy us. Materialism, consumerism, and influencers who emphasize what feels good rather than obedience to Christ, they are all ploys of the enemy to lead our hearts away from the source of all that is good.

How are we to combat these sweet deceptions except by steeping our minds in what is good and true? The entire book of Psalms tells us that God is good and only does good; shouldn't it be God we seek to learn from? Let's accept the challenge today to note what seemingly good things are being influential at a personal level. How do they compare to the truth of Scripture?

REFLECTION

Have you been swayed by things that look and sound good but are really empty? How can you fill up on the truth of God's Word, so you are not tempted to binge on lesser things?

MY THOUGHTS

After reflecting on this devotion and follow-up questions, here are my thoughts.

MY RESPONSE

This is how I can apply the message to my life.

"There is only One who is good."

MATTHEW 19:17 NIV

To me, this Scripture feels most like (check one)

☐ A PROMISE ☐ AN INSTRUCTION ☐ A TRUTH

Here's how it impacts me...

PRAYER

GRATITUDE

I have been blessed with so many good things.
Here is what I am particularly thankful for this week.

REQUESTS

After reading and reflecting, here is what I'm asking God for.

WEEK 4

Courage

LORD, you are my shield,
my wonderful God who gives me courage.
I will pray to the LORD,
and he will answer me from his holy mountain.

PSALM 3:3-4 NCV

As a child or young adult, courage might seem like something called upon for great, meaningful accomplishments like saving someone from drowning. But as we grow older, we learn that courage is most necessary when life's pressures mount, struggle knocks on the door, or the burden of pain causes our shoulders to slump. It is not only in the life-altering moments of heroism when we need courage. We will call on it the mornings after a fight with a friend, when a family member uses words like knives, the day our job lets us go, or when depression creeps in.

On these days, it is vital to remember the source of our strength. It is imperative that we do not shut the door to block out the world without first turning our gaze heavenward. On these days we must lay hold of the courage that our wonderful God offers us. We can lift up our heads because our help is on the way even before we pray.

Reflection

Life is sweet when you trust in Jesus. Regardless of your struggle, he is with you. He is the source of your courage and joy. What do you need courage for today?

MY THOUGHTS

After reflecting on this devotion and follow-up questions, here are my thoughts.

MY RESPONSE

This is how I can apply the message to my life.

*You are my refuge
and my shield;
I have put my hope
in your word.*

PSALM 119:114 NIV

To me, this Scripture feels most like (check one)

☐ A PROMISE ☐ AN INSTRUCTION ☐ A TRUTH

Here's how it impacts me...

PRAYER

GRATITUDE

I have been blessed with so many good things.
Here is what I am particularly thankful for this week.

REQUESTS

After reading and reflecting, here is what I'm asking God for.

WEEK 5

Made Righteous

> As for me, by Your abundant graciousness
> I will enter Your house,
> At Your holy temple
> I will bow in reverence for You.
>
> PSALM 5:7 NASB

No one is perfect; we all have our flaws and secret sins. It is easy to see the unrighteousness of those who lead wicked lives, who boast about evil, or take pleasure in wrongdoing. When we compare ourselves to those who are outwardly immoral, we tend to feel that we are doing a pretty good job. In reality, sin is sin, and no one is righteous in his own merit. But what grace has been extended to those of us who have trusted Jesus. Because we are covered in the blood of Christ, the Father sees us as righteous and welcomes us as if we have done no wrong.

We each can thank Jesus for his abundant grace. We deserved death, but God in his mercy brought us into his house. Today, when we see the depravity of the world around us and we are tempted to consider ourselves virtuous, remember that it is only by the sweet grace of Christ that we can draw near to God.

Reflection

God is so gracious. Thank him for covering you in righteousness. How can you live with a thankful spirit in this moment?

MY THOUGHTS

After reflecting on this devotion and follow-up questions, here are my thoughts.

MY RESPONSE

This is how I can apply the message to my life.

Let's go to his dwelling place;
let's worship at his footstool.

PSALM 132:7 CSB

To me, this Scripture feels most like (check one)

☐ A PROMISE ☐ AN INSTRUCTION ☐ A TRUTH

Here's how it impacts me…

PRAYER

GRATITUDE

I have been blessed with so many good things.
Here is what I am particularly thankful for this week.

REQUESTS

After reading and reflecting, here is what I'm asking God for.

WEEK 6

True Love

Let your unfailing love surround us, Lord,
for our hope is in you alone.

Psalm 33:22 NLT

Chick flicks and rom coms have long given us a definition of love which modern women cling to in their search for romance. Love is willing to chase us through the airport to stop our flight. Love will give up hopes and dreams in order to fulfill ours. Love will deny family relationships in order to pursue one true love. Rarely, if ever, do we see a display of love that goes beyond the initial attraction and pursuit.

This sets us up for misunderstanding real love, but it's time to set things straight. Real love is quieter but no less extraordinary. Real love is faithful. Real love continues to show up despite our inadequacies. Real love sees the best and the worst and chooses to accept both. Real love allows room for mistakes, growth, and setbacks; it always hopes for better. Real love is Christ.

Reflection

Jesus demonstrated true love—love that is unfailing, everlasting, always patient, and always hopeful. How have you assumed that love is only loud and bold? Where do you see beauty in God's quiet, faithful love?

MY THOUGHTS

After reflecting on this devotion and follow-up questions, here are my thoughts.

MY RESPONSE

This is how I can apply the message to my life.

I have trusted
in your faithful love;
my heart will rejoice
in your deliverance.

PSALM 13:5 CSB

To me, this Scripture feels most like (check one)

☐ A PROMISE ☐ AN INSTRUCTION ☐ A TRUTH

Here's how it impacts me...

Prayer

GRATITUDE

I have been blessed with so many good things.
Here is what I am particularly thankful for this week.

REQUESTS

After reading and reflecting, here is what I'm asking God for.

WEEK 7

Trustworthy

Everything he does is good and fair;
all his orders can be trusted.

PSALM 111:7 NCV

In today's world, maybe more than ever before, doubt is everywhere. We suspect everyone and everything; wariness always precedes believing the best of someone. It is no surprise, then, that our view of God's Word and his call to us as believers is also met with hesitation.

Scripture could not be clearer about the trustworthiness of God and his Word. Imagine knowing someone who always did what was right and good, brought comfort in the midst of trial, found the good in every situation, and followed through on every single promise. That is our God. He is completely good, and his Word is entirely trustworthy. Is he asking you to do something about which you have been uncertain? Has he called you to action, but you've been doubtful that he'll see you through? Hesitate no more!

REFLECTION

You can trust God completely. Don't doubt his Word. How can you depend on his goodness to lead you today?

MY THOUGHTS

After reflecting on this devotion and follow-up questions, here are my thoughts.

MY RESPONSE

This is how I can apply the message to my life.

The Rock, his work is perfect,
for all his ways are justice.

DEUTERONOMY 32:4 ESV

To me, this Scripture feels most like (check one)

☐ A PROMISE ☐ AN INSTRUCTION ☐ A TRUTH

Here's how it impacts me…

PRAYER

GRATITUDE

I have been blessed with so many good things.
Here is what I am particularly thankful for this week.

REQUESTS

After reading and reflecting, here is what I'm asking God for.

WEEK 8

Grace in Every Season

My soul clings to the dust;
give me life according to your word!

PSALM 119:25 ESV

Life can be heavy. For the Christian, hard times are guaranteed. We have days when our souls feel dragged through the dust, when our lungs just can't seem to breathe in enough air. Those days, or weeks, or months can drag on until we have lost all hope. It is not easy to say or easy to hear, but it is vital to understand that those times are a form of grace.

When life is simple, pleasant, or straightforward, we tend to think that it is our own capability which has caused things to level out for us. We forget that we are but a vapor and our entire existence is dependent on the Creator's mercy. When the burdens begin to stack up, when our backs and hearts break under the pressure, it is then in that painful grace-filled season, that we remember who sustains us. If life is heavy today, cry out as the psalmist did for life according to his Word. He promises to strengthen you.

REFLECTION

Every season of life is full of God's grace. Ask him for strength for today as you trust in him.

MY THOUGHTS

After reflecting on this devotion and follow-up questions, here are my thoughts.

MY RESPONSE

This is how I can apply the message to my life.

Set your minds on the things that are above, not on the things that are on earth.

COLOSSIANS 3:2 NASB

To me, this Scripture feels most like (check one)

☐ A PROMISE ☐ AN INSTRUCTION ☐ A TRUTH

Here's how it impacts me...

....

....

....

....

....

PRAYER

GRATITUDE

I have been blessed with so many good things.
Here is what I am particularly thankful for this week.

REQUESTS

After reading and reflecting, here is what I'm asking God for.

WEEK 9

Godly Life

> His divine power has given us everything we need for a godly life through our knowledge of him who called us by his own glory and goodness.
>
> 2 PETER 1:3 NIV

Perhaps you woke up this morning unprepared for the day. You slept poorly, your project deadline got moved up, and the coffee maker wouldn't work. You want nothing more than to return to bed and hit the restart button. But life awaits. How will you respond? It is tempting to think that on those days God understands our angst and will surely tolerate a less-than-ideal attitude.

We know better. Peter tells us that God's divine power has given us *everything* we need for living a godly life. This isn't just on the days when we get enough sleep and coffee; it's maybe specifically on the days when everything seems to go wrong. By his goodness we have been called, not to get by with our teeth clenched and our hearts set on the end of this awful day. Instead, we have been called to live a life of humility, patience, self-sacrifice, and joy. This is how Jesus lived. Take a moment and ask for God's grace to live a godly life today.

REFLECTION

God has given you everything you need not just to endure the day but to make it sweet. What does choosing joy look like today?

MY THOUGHTS

After reflecting on this devotion and follow-up questions, here are my thoughts.

MY RESPONSE

This is how I can apply the message to my life.

"My grace is sufficient for you, for power is perfected in weakness."

2 CORINTHIANS 12:9 NASB

To me, this Scripture feels most like (check one)

☐ A PROMISE ☐ AN INSTRUCTION ☐ A TRUTH

Here's how it impacts me...

PRAYER

GRATITUDE

I have been blessed with so many good things.
Here is what I am particularly thankful for this week.

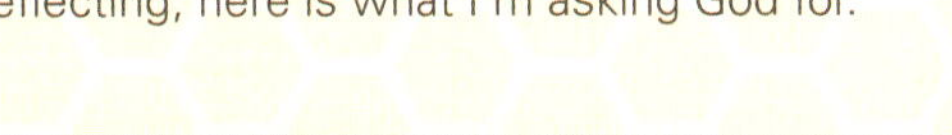

REQUESTS

After reading and reflecting, here is what I'm asking God for.

WEEK 10

Refuge

> Taste and see that the Lord is good.
> Oh, the joys of those who take refuge in him!
>
> PSALM 34:8 NLT

What do you take refuge in? We all have something. Maybe for you it is a good workout to burn away the day's stress, or the time at night when everything is quiet, or perhaps it is the accolades you receive on social media. A refuge is a safe place—a place where we run and hide from the troubles of our lives. But what happens when the very thing we count on as our safe place is unavailable?

Scripture tells us to taste and see—to experience with our senses and with our whole being—that the Lord is good. He is a good place to hide ourselves when things are getting tough. His refuge offers peace for our minds and joy for our hearts. It is not dependent on things going a certain way; it cannot be taken from us when the day takes unexpected turns. We need to check our hearts today and make sure we are hiding ourselves in the certainty of Christ.

REFLECTION

What created things do you rely on to relieve your stress and bring you joy? True and lasting joy is only found in God. How will you take hold of that today?

MY THOUGHTS

After reflecting on this devotion and follow-up questions, here are my thoughts.

MY RESPONSE

This is how I can apply the message to my life.

Your promises
are sweet to me,
sweeter than honey
in my mouth!

PSALM 119:103 NCV

To me, this Scripture feels most like (check one)

☐ A PROMISE ☐ AN INSTRUCTION ☐ A TRUTH

Here's how it impacts me...

PRAYER

GRATITUDE

I have been blessed with so many good things.
Here is what I am particularly thankful for this week.

REQUESTS

After reading and reflecting, here is what I'm asking God for.

WEEK 11

Always Faithful

"The LORD, the LORD, a God merciful and gracious, slow to anger, and abounding in steadfast love and faithfulness, keeping steadfast love for thousands, forgiving iniquity and transgression and sin."

EXODUS 34:6-7 ESV

Close your eyes for a moment and think back on the last month of your life. Consider the hard days and the good days and think about them in light of God's faithfulness. What stands out to you? Does his faithfulness make itself known in extraordinary and loud ways, like the parting of the Red Sea? Or does it barely come through, like a light that seeps out through a crack in the door?

God's faithfulness, we are told, is abounding. That doesn't always mean it's flashy and audacious. Sometimes it is the quiet but sustaining force that carries us through a dark season. We might not even be aware of it until after the fact. But the reality is that we are never without it. Thank you, God for your abounding faithfulness in our lives.

Reflection

How has God proven himself faithful in your life? Have you failed to recognize it? Today, be more aware of the ways he extends his faithfulness and love to you.

MY THOUGHTS

After reflecting on this devotion and follow-up questions, here are my thoughts.

MY RESPONSE

This is how I can apply the message to my life.

The Lord is kind
and shows mercy.
He does not become angry
quickly but is full of love.

PSALM 145:8 NCV

To me, this Scripture feels most like (check one)

☐ A PROMISE ☐ AN INSTRUCTION ☐ A TRUTH

Here's how it impacts me...

....

....

....

....

....

Prayer

GRATITUDE

I have been blessed with so many good things.
Here is what I am particularly thankful for this week.

REQUESTS

After reading and reflecting, here is what I'm asking God for.

WEEK 12

Freedom

> I will live in freedom,
> because I want to follow your orders.
>
> PSALM 119:45 NCV

As a young adult, Heather couldn't wait for the day when she lived on her own and made her own rules. She longed for freedom to make plans and follow her dreams. When she was twenty-two years old, she was finally out on her own and tasting the freedom she had yearned for. It wasn't long, however, before she realized that life on her own didn't hold the fulfillment that she had assumed it would. Her actions held consequences, and she began to understand that it wasn't freedom from rules or authority that she needed.

Heather began to appreciate Scripture which gives guidelines for how life works best. She saw wisdom in God's instructions: how they provided protection, gave advice for tough situations, and spoke of God's mercy that always attended her even in her mistakes. Freedom, she found, was not in independence and making her own rules; it was found in bowing to Christ and discovering the peaceful sovereignty by which her life was ruled.

Reflection

Do you insist on doing things your own way? Remember that freedom is found in your obedience to God's Word which speaks of his desire for your best life.

MY THOUGHTS

After reflecting on this devotion and follow-up questions, here are my thoughts.

MY RESPONSE

This is how I can apply the message to my life.

Don't act thoughtlessly,
but understand what
the Lord wants you to do.

EPHESIANS 5:17 NLT

To me, this Scripture feels most like (check one)

☐ A PROMISE ☐ AN INSTRUCTION ☐ A TRUTH

Here's how it impacts me...

PRAYER

GRATITUDE

I have been blessed with so many good things.
Here is what I am particularly thankful for this week.

REQUESTS

After reading and reflecting, here is what I'm asking God for.

WEEK 13

Feast for the Soul

> You satisfy me more than the richest feast.
> I will praise you with songs of joy.
>
> PSALM 63:5 NLT

It's amazing to have a satisfying meal after a long day of hard work. Our bodies were made for nourishment, and they work best when they are regularly fed with good, nutrient-rich food. Similarly, our souls were not made to fast for extended periods of time; we need regular nourishment from the source of life—Jesus. Just like a feast at the richest of celebrations which offers all the good things we could want to eat, Jesus eases the pangs of hunger that our souls experience living in this world.

We are constantly looking for ways to fulfill our longing for more, but the created world was never meant to satiate our thirst. What things are you pursuing to fill you? Make sure you are giving your soul regular nourishment by spending time in the Word and in prayer with your heavenly Father. You will be satisfied.

Reflection

Jesus, thank you for satisfying my longings with your presence and your joy. Forgive me for seeking other things to fill the void in my heart and help me pursue you alone.

MY THOUGHTS

After reflecting on this devotion and follow-up questions, here are my thoughts.

MY RESPONSE

This is how I can apply the message to my life.

What joy for those you choose to bring near, those who live in your holy courts.

PSALM 65:4 NLT

To me, this Scripture feels most like (check one)

☐ A PROMISE ☐ AN INSTRUCTION ☐ A TRUTH

Here's how it impacts me...

Prayer

GRATITUDE

I have been blessed with so many good things.
Here is what I am particularly thankful for this week.

REQUESTS

After reading and reflecting, here is what I'm asking God for.

WEEK 14

Welcomed Home

Do not turn away from me.
Do not turn your servant away in anger;
you have helped me.
Do not push me away or leave me alone,
God, my Savior.

PSALM 27:9 NCV

Have you ever experienced the silent treatment? Angry friends or loved ones can push us away when we have hurt them, refusing to speak to us when we desperately want connection and reconciliation. Perhaps you've been the one to refuse a restored relationship at times in your life. When we have sinned against God, it is natural to think that he will respond with the same anger that we have received in our lives from others. We're expecting to be pushed away and received with stony silence when we plea for reconciliation.

But what mercy is ours when we approach his throne of grace! Instead of anger, we find love. Instead of God shunning us, we find his open arms. Instead of abandoning our friendship, we find him rejoicing to restore our relationship. God's mercy is waiting for us to return.

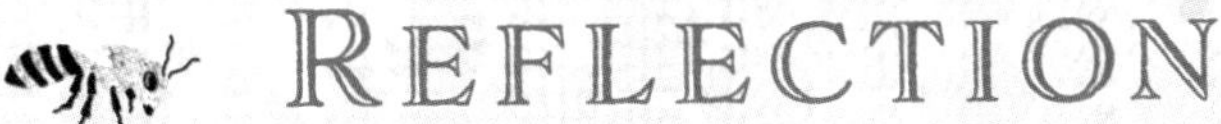

REFLECTION

God is merciful and good. Thank him for never getting tired of welcoming you back. His patience does not wear thin. How can you walk in righteousness today?

MY THOUGHTS

After reflecting on this devotion and follow-up questions, here are my thoughts.

MY RESPONSE

This is how I can apply the message to my life.

Don't hide your face
from your servant,
for I am in distress.
Answer me quickly!

PSALM 69:17 CSB

To me, this Scripture feels most like (check one)

☐ A PROMISE ☐ AN INSTRUCTION ☐ A TRUTH

Here's how it impacts me...

PRAYER

GRATITUDE

I have been blessed with so many good things.
Here is what I am particularly thankful for this week.

REQUESTS

After reading and reflecting, here is what I'm asking God for.

WEEK 15

Hurrying Back to God

I thought about my life,
and I decided to follow your rules.
I hurried and did not wait
to obey your commands.

PSALM 119:59-60 NCV

Imagine you went hiking in the Rocky Mountains. The path was winding and beautiful, and you were overcome with wonder as you traversed the trail. But suddenly you realized you were no longer on the path. Somewhere along the way you must have missed a turn, and now you are lost. You certainly would not hesitate in turning back in order to find the trail. You wouldn't say to yourself, "I've come this far, I'll just go a little further before turning around."

Now think about your spiritual life. When you realize you are not walking in righteousness, how quickly do you turn back to the Lord? Oftentimes shame, pride, or sinful desires keep you from hurrying back to God. But dangers lie in wait when you do not turn in haste from your sin. Just as darkness can prevent you from getting to safety on a mountain trail, it can also put you in a dangerous place when you hesitate to come back to God.

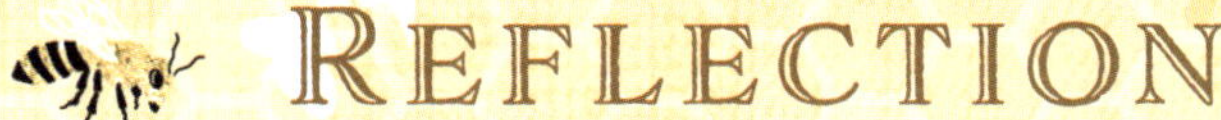

REFLECTION

Are you hesitating to repent and return to God? What are you struggling to give up? God will not meet you with a heavy hand. He has abundant mercy for you. Thank him for his mercy and grace today.

MY THOUGHTS

After reflecting on this devotion and follow-up questions, here are my thoughts.

MY RESPONSE

This is how I can apply the message to my life.

Let us test and
examine our ways,
and return to the Lord!

LAMENTATIONS 3:40 ESV

To me, this Scripture feels most like (check one)

☐ A PROMISE ☐ AN INSTRUCTION ☐ A TRUTH

Here's how it impacts me...

Prayer

GRATITUDE

I have been blessed with so many good things.
Here is what I am particularly thankful for this week.

REQUESTS

After reading and reflecting, here is what I'm asking God for.

WEEK 16

Governed by Goodness

> The LORD is good to everyone.
> He showers compassion on all his creation.
>
> PSALM 145:9 NLT

You might have a basic understanding of God's goodness, but does it affect the way you live? God's nature causes him to be good to all mankind. He sends rain on the just and the unjust. He is compassionate, kind, and merciful. He is patient and does not want anyone to perish; he is hoping for all to repent.

Hopefully, the awareness of God's goodness causes a spirit of humility to rise up in you; hopefully it inspires you to extend the same goodness to others. It may allow you to see the body of Christ as well as those whose hearts are far from God with the same level of compassion, breathing out kindness to those who love you as well as those who persecute you. It will hopefully cause you to repent from sin and return to God with joy, being confident that he will receive you back as if you had never sinned.

REFLECTION

God's goodness can change you from the inside out. How does this knowledge change the way you live? What are the implications of God's divine attributes in your life?

MY THOUGHTS

After reflecting on this devotion and follow-up questions, here are my thoughts.

MY RESPONSE

This is how I can apply the message to my life.

The Lord is not slow to fulfill his promise as some count slowness, but is patient toward you, not wishing that any should perish, but that all should reach repentance.

2 PETER 3:9 ESV

To me, this Scripture feels most like (check one)

☐ A PROMISE ☐ AN INSTRUCTION ☐ A TRUTH

Here's how it impacts me...

....

....

....

....

....

Prayer

GRATITUDE

I have been blessed with so many good things.
Here is what I am particularly thankful for this week.

REQUESTS

After reading and reflecting, here is what I'm asking God for.

WEEK 17

Source of Joy

> Those who sing as well as those
> who play the flutes will say,
> "All my springs of joy are in You."
>
> PSALM 87:7 NASB

Any one of us could tell the next person how life is a series of ups and downs. The highest highs and the lowest lows weave together to form the messy tapestry of life. As followers of Christ, it is important that we see each moment—wonderful or tragic—as an opportunity to praise God for being our source of joy. Today, are you embracing where Christ has you, allowing him to shape your character and your story according to his will? Or are you waiting for things to change, to improve, to be the green grass of a happy life that someone else already seems to have?

Consider how you are viewing your life and ask yourself if you are connected to the source of your joy. Allow yourself to repent of longing for an earthly utopia and embrace your present situation. Embrace the fact that Jesus is enough for you even when nothing else is.

Reflection

If Jesus is all you have, you have it all. He can be your source of joy in all seasons of life. What are some of your highest highs in life? How have you seen God's hand in your lows?

MY THOUGHTS

After reflecting on this devotion and follow-up questions, here are my thoughts.

MY RESPONSE

This is how I can apply the message to my life.

With you is the fountain of life; in your light we see light.

PSALM 36:9 NIV

To me, this Scripture feels most like (check one)

☐ A PROMISE ☐ AN INSTRUCTION ☐ A TRUTH

Here's how it impacts me...

....

....

....

....

....

PRAYER

GRATITUDE

I have been blessed with so many good things.
Here is what I am particularly thankful for this week.

REQUESTS

After reading and reflecting, here is what I'm asking God for.

WEEK 18

Rights or Promises

> Let us hold fast the confession of our hope without wavering, for he who promised is faithful.
>
> HEBREWS 10:23 ESV

Gigi was peeved. The restful night of sleep she longed for had once again evaded her for no apparent reason. Here she was serving in ministry, sacrificing herself in order to bring others into the family of faith, and she couldn't even get a full night's sleep. She was annoyed with God. Where were his blessings? She sulked through her day, but the Spirit wouldn't let her get away with her complaining. She finally realized that she was clinging to good sleep as if it were something she was entitled to. She had turned it into a right, something which had never been promised.

In that moment she repented and began to count the things of God which are promised to her: the love of God that cannot be removed, abundant life, the care of the Father, a purpose in life that will be fulfilled according to his will, and that all of God's promises to his people are a resounding yes in Christ.

REFLECTION

You can trust God's promises because he is faithful. What things are you holding fast to that were never promised? What does it look like to cling to that which God has promised?

MY THOUGHTS

After reflecting on this devotion and follow-up questions, here are my thoughts.

MY RESPONSE

This is how I can apply the message to my life.

The Lord is faithful,
and he will strengthen you
and protect you
from the evil one.

2 THESSALONIANS 3:3 NIV

To me, this Scripture feels most like (check one)

☐ A PROMISE ☐ AN INSTRUCTION ☐ A TRUTH

Here's how it impacts me...

....

....

....

....

....

Prayer

GRATITUDE

I have been blessed with so many good things.
Here is what I am particularly thankful for this week.

REQUESTS

After reading and reflecting, here is what I'm asking God for.

WEEK 19

Foundation

Before the mountains were born
and before you created the earth and the world,
you are God.
You have always been,
and you will always be.

PSALM 90:2 NCV

How you perceive God will impact you and the way you live your life. We know what God is like because of what Scripture says, because of the Spirit living in us, and because of the body of Christ who helps us grasp his character. But what is your understanding of God really based on?

It is all too easy to comprehend God through the lens of our human experience, allowing that lens to define God for us. This might cause us to see him as someone who withholds good from us or who loves us based on what we do or who is untrustworthy. All of these notions are false according to Scripture and will lead us to an understanding of God that is not right. Check the foundation for your comprehension of God, and make sure it is based upon truth.

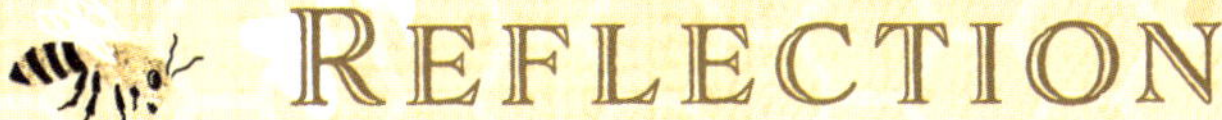

REFLECTION

Is your heart's understanding of God based upon the truth of his Word or on limited human experience? What can you do to ensure your view is not tainted by the world?

MY THOUGHTS

After reflecting on this devotion and follow-up questions, here are my thoughts.

MY RESPONSE

This is how I can apply the message to my life.

"Turn to Me and be saved,
all the ends of the earth;
For I am God,
and there is no other."

ISAIAH 45:22 NASB

To me, this Scripture feels most like (check one)

☐ A PROMISE ☐ AN INSTRUCTION ☐ A TRUTH

Here's how it impacts me...

PRAYER

GRATITUDE

I have been blessed with so many good things.
Here is what I am particularly thankful for this week.

REQUESTS

After reading and reflecting, here is what I'm asking God for.

WEEK 20

Sovereign Goodness

> We know that God causes all things to work together for good to those who love God, to those who are called according to His purpose.
>
> ROMANS 8:28 NASB

Human life is full of conflict. From birth, our stories are built on overcoming conflict or bending and breaking as a result of it. Perhaps today you find yourself in a battle and you are struggling to perceive the blessing that will come from it. But as believers we must have faith that there is no battle we will face which will not produce some good.

Do you believe strongly in the sovereignty and goodness of God? Do you rise to the occasion when conflict occurs, waiting with anticipation for how God will show his goodness? Or do you avoid trouble at all costs and then panic when it finds you? Here is something to remember: if you belong to God, you cannot lose. Regardless of your battle, you are sure to win if you are on God's side.

Reflection

You are not alone in your struggles. God knew your battles before he created everything, and he knew the blessings that would arise from them according to his sovereign goodness. How will you trust in that today?

MY THOUGHTS

After reflecting on this devotion and follow-up questions, here are my thoughts.

MY RESPONSE

This is how I can apply the message to my life.

No temptation has overtaken you except what is common to mankind. And God is faithful; he will not let you be tempted beyond what you can bear.

1 CORINTHIANS 10:13 NIV

To me, this Scripture feels most like (check one)

☐ A PROMISE ☐ AN INSTRUCTION ☐ A TRUTH

Here's how it impacts me...

Prayer

GRATITUDE

I have been blessed with so many good things.
Here is what I am particularly thankful for this week.

REQUESTS

After reading and reflecting, here is what I'm asking God for.

WEEK 21

Weakness of Resolve

> The one who calls you is faithful,
> and he will do it.
>
> 1 THESSALONIANS 5:24 NIV

We have certainly all resolved to make things happen in our lives. Maybe for you it is a resolve to create a life that is different than the one you had growing up. Perhaps it is to fit into a certain clothing size or to reach the top of your company. Determination can be a noble trait, but there are certain things that we will never attain through resolve alone. Holiness is one of those.

We cannot will away our sinful nature, nor determine that we will reach perfection. It is only through the faithful work of the Holy Spirit in our lives and our willingness to hear and obey that we will ever reach sanctification.

If you have been trying in your own willpower to please God, or to overcome a recurring sin, or maybe to see freedom from addiction, you will only find yourself worn out, defeated, and ready to give up. Cry out to your faithful God; he will help you.

Reflection

What are you determined to see happen in your life? God has not left you on your own to reach holiness. He is faithful to help you.

MY THOUGHTS

After reflecting on this devotion and follow-up questions, here are my thoughts.

MY RESPONSE

This is how I can apply the message to my life.

It is God who works in you to will and to act in order to fulfill his good purpose.

PHILIPPIANS 2:13 NIV

To me, this Scripture feels most like (check one)

☐ A PROMISE ☐ AN INSTRUCTION ☐ A TRUTH

Here's how it impacts me...

PRAYER

GRATITUDE

I have been blessed with so many good things.
Here is what I am particularly thankful for this week.

REQUESTS

After reading and reflecting, here is what I'm asking God for.

WEEK 22

Faithful Joy

> We do this by keeping our eyes on Jesus, the champion who initiates and perfects our faith. Because of the joy awaiting him, he endured the cross, disregarding its shame. Now he is seated in the place of honor beside God's throne.
>
> HEBREWS 12:2 NLT

Jesus knew what it meant to suffer in life. In all the things he faced throughout his ministry leading to his death on the cross, he was faithful. Life for him, as it is for all of us, was not rainbows and butterflies; it was a challenge. It was dealing with people who scorned him and didn't believe in his goodness. In the end, they had him killed for being the best.

In all of this, Jesus did not lose sight of the promise the Father gave him: his sheep that would be rescued as a result of his life and death. He showed us how to live a life of steadfastness and joy in the midst of difficulty.

REFLECTION

How can you choose not to be dragged along by life but to stand tall, strong, and joyful in the midst of monotony, sleeplessness, gray days, or a demanding job? How do you keep from living a defeated life?

MY THOUGHTS

After reflecting on this devotion and follow-up questions, here are my thoughts.

MY RESPONSE

This is how I can apply the message to my life.

"I will look to
the Lord for help.
I will wait for
God to save me;
my God will hear me."

MICAH 7:7 NCV

To me, this Scripture feels most like (check one)

☐ A PROMISE ☐ AN INSTRUCTION ☐ A TRUTH

Here's how it impacts me...

Prayer

GRATITUDE

I have been blessed with so many good things.
Here is what I am particularly thankful for this week.

REQUESTS

After reading and reflecting, here is what I'm asking God for.

WEEK 23

Ever True

> Your kingdom is an everlasting kingdom,
> and your dominion endures
> throughout all generations.
> The LORD is faithful in all his words
> and kind in all his works.
>
> PSALM 145:13 ESV

That fact that God is faithful rests entirely on his immutability. If God cannot change, then the concept of his faithfulness is completely secure and to be trusted entirely. If God cannot change, then every promise he has made is sure to stand. If God cannot change, we can live with the peaceful knowledge that he will never remove his love from us. If God cannot change, then we know that his kindness will continue to be extended to those who love God and walk in righteousness.

God is ever true to himself and to his Word. This ought to encourage our hearts today in the confidence of God's Word. Very little in this world is true even when we are led to believe it is. But Scripture is true! Let's fill our hearts and minds with truth today, so that we are ready to discern the lies of the enemy and to stand firm in the knowledge of God's perfect faithfulness.

REFLECTION

How are you comforted by knowing that the promises of God are secure? You can trust his Word completely and find confidence in arming yourself with it as you face difficulties.

MY THOUGHTS

After reflecting on this devotion and follow-up questions, here are my thoughts.

MY RESPONSE

This is how I can apply the message to my life.

He was given dominion
and glory and a kingdom,
so that those of every people,
nation, and language
should serve him.

DANIEL 7:14 CSB

To me, this Scripture feels most like (check one)

☐ A PROMISE ☐ AN INSTRUCTION ☐ A TRUTH

Here's how it impacts me...

PRAYER

GRATITUDE

I have been blessed with so many good things.
Here is what I am particularly thankful for this week.

REQUESTS

After reading and reflecting, here is what I'm asking God for.

WEEK 24

Satisfied by Sacred

> Because I am righteous, I will see you.
> When I awake, I will see you face to face
> and be satisfied.
>
> PSALM 17:15 NLT

We were created to yearn for the one who fills the void in our souls and stops the ache in our hearts. All of human life is spent attempting to fill the emptiness within, and it doesn't stop once we have found Jesus. Unfortunately, our hearts are still prone to seek fulfillment in other things, and it is a constant battle to find ourselves satisfied in Christ.

We can tell what things we are looking to fill us by asking the question, "What is sacred to me?" When we find it difficult to give these things up, then we know that we are not finding our satisfaction in Jesus. It's often the case that too many other things are clouding our viewpoints. Likes on social media, dressing well, or having nice things may be some of our sacred things. When we begin to give these up, we find that we can actually see Jesus. And when we see Jesus, nothing else will matter.

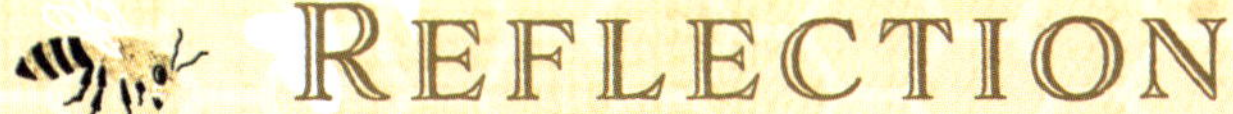

REFLECTION

What is clouding your view of God? What can you set aside that has become sacred to you?

MY THOUGHTS

After reflecting on this devotion and follow-up questions, here are my thoughts.

MY RESPONSE

This is how I can apply the message to my life.

"Blessed are those who hunger and thirst for righteousness, for they shall be satisfied."

MATTHEW 5:6 ESV

To me, this Scripture feels most like (check one)

☐ A PROMISE ☐ AN INSTRUCTION ☐ A TRUTH

Here's how it impacts me...

....

....

....

....

....

PRAYER

GRATITUDE

I have been blessed with so many good things.
Here is what I am particularly thankful for this week.

REQUESTS

After reading and reflecting, here is what I'm asking God for.

WEEK 25

Extend Grace

> May God be gracious to us and bless us
> and make his face to shine upon us,
> that your way may be known on earth,
> your saving power among all nations.
>
> PSALM 67:1-2 ESV

God's grace abounds to those who belong to him. The manifestation of his grace in our lives is not just so we can be called his favored ones but so his salvation can be shown to the world. It is easy to accept his blessing, but it can be harder to accept his call to bless others. If we truly believe that God has been gracious to us, then we will become gracious to the people God puts in our lives.

Is that reflected in your life today? Are you sitting pretty on the blessings of God but neglecting to ask him how you can now be a blessing by extending his grace to those around you? Whether it is toward your family, friends, coworkers, neighbors, or even strangers, ask the Lord what it means to give grace as you have received. Do not allow yourself to know his blessings without also blessing the world around you.

Reflection

You are a recipient of God's grace. How can you choose not to settle comfortably into that favor but be moved into action? How can you be a blessing to others?

MY THOUGHTS

After reflecting on this devotion and follow-up questions, here are my thoughts.

MY RESPONSE

This is how I can apply the message to my life.

Let your face smile on us, Lord.

PSALM 4:6 NLT

To me, this Scripture feels most like (check one)

☐ A PROMISE ☐ AN INSTRUCTION ☐ A TRUTH

Here's how it impacts me...

Prayer

GRATITUDE

I have been blessed with so many good things.
Here is what I am particularly thankful for this week.

REQUESTS

After reading and reflecting, here is what I'm asking God for.

WEEK 26

Waiting

> Wait patiently for the LORD.
> Be brave and courageous.
> Yes, wait patiently for the LORD.
>
> PSALM 27:14 NLT

Waiting is no one's favorite pastime. Waiting causes us to collide with our lack of patience. It goes against our natural desire to get what we want when we want it, and it shows us our lack of control. While we can't usually change our circumstances to make the waiting period shorter, we can keep seeking the Lord while we wait.

Are you in a season of waiting? It can be challenging to wake up every day still lacking what you desire. But you will never be disappointed if you continue to go to God day after day while you wait for the fulfillment of your dream. Waiting is never the only thing to do for the believer. Wake up each morning and act upon your knowledge of God's grace because you belong to him. Wake up and praise him for his goodness to you today. Wake up and seek his heart for the people around you. You will not be disappointed.

REFLECTION

What are you waiting for? While you wait, you have hope for the promise of good things. How can you seek God and not get caught up waiting for what's to come? What gifts are in front of you today?

MY THOUGHTS

After reflecting on this devotion and follow-up questions, here are my thoughts.

MY RESPONSE

This is how I can apply the message to my life.

*Put your hope in the Lord.
Travel steadily along
his path.*

PSALM 37:34 NLT

To me, this Scripture feels most like (check one)

☐ A PROMISE ☐ AN INSTRUCTION ☐ A TRUTH

Here's how it impacts me...

....

....

....

....

....

PRAYER

GRATITUDE

I have been blessed with so many good things.
Here is what I am particularly thankful for this week.

REQUESTS

After reading and reflecting, here is what I'm asking God for.

WEEK 27

Too Good

> They will burst forth in speaking of your abundant goodness, and will shout joyfully of your righteousness.
>
> PSALM 145:7 NASB

Scripture tells us to declare God's goodness and to sing of his righteousness. Have you done that lately? It is all too easy to fall into the rut of trudging through the monotony of daily life without taking time to acknowledge God's goodness in our ordinary days.

What does his goodness look like for you today? Did you get some quiet time early in the day? Was there sunshine after the stormy weather? Did you have an answer to prayer? Did you get to spend time with an encouraging friend? Signs of God's goodness surround your daily life; are you open to seeing it and declaring it? Do not let this day go by without taking the opportunity to burst forth in speaking about God's abundant goodness, just as the psalmist wrote.

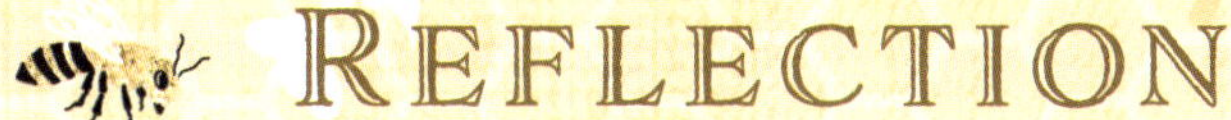

Reflection

God's goodness is worth sharing with others. Write your personal account of God's goodness. How is he declaring his love even in the smallest things?

MY THOUGHTS

After reflecting on this devotion and follow-up questions, here are my thoughts.

MY RESPONSE

This is how I can apply the message to my life.

I will tell how
you do what is right.
I will tell about your
salvation all day long,
even though it is
more than I can tell.

PSALM 71:15 NCV

To me, this Scripture feels most like (check one)

☐ A PROMISE ☐ AN INSTRUCTION ☐ A TRUTH

Here's how it impacts me...

PRAYER

GRATITUDE

I have been blessed with so many good things.
Here is what I am particularly thankful for this week.

REQUESTS

After reading and reflecting, here is what I'm asking God for.

WEEK 28

Grace Between

> Surely goodness and mercy shall follow me
> all the days of my life,
> and I shall dwell in the house of the LORD
> forever.
>
> PSALM 23:6 ESV

What grace can you find in your day today? Some days everything seems to go wrong all at once; you break your finger, your car gets a flat on the way to the doctor, and you didn't get the promotion you were hoping for. Life has a way of storing up all its troubles, so they tumble down all at once.

We do not have to be consumed by all the bad news. When a torrent of troubles hits all at once, we can find grace woven between the grief. What good things can we see and praise God for when life is throwing us curveballs? We are guaranteed to rise above the fog of despair that tends to settle on these hard days if we keep our gaze focused on the grace God promises. It follows us all the way through life. Psalm 23 is a beautiful song about God's amazing promise to us.

REFLECTION

When everything seems to be going wrong, how do you keep your grace perspective?

MY THOUGHTS

After reflecting on this devotion and follow-up questions, here are my thoughts.

MY RESPONSE

This is how I can apply the message to my life.

You make known to me
the path of life;
you will fill me with joy
in your presence.

PSALM 16:11 NIV

To me, this Scripture feels most like (check one)

☐ A PROMISE ☐ AN INSTRUCTION ☐ A TRUTH

Here's how it impacts me…

....

....

....

....

....

Prayer

GRATITUDE

I have been blessed with so many good things.
Here is what I am particularly thankful for this week.

REQUESTS

After reading and reflecting, here is what I'm asking God for.

WEEK 29

Unfailing Love

Your unfailing love is better than life itself;
how I praise you!

PSALM 63:3 NLT

God's love is unfailing. It's hard to grasp since our minds are held to the confines of our flawed human understanding and experiences. Never in our lives have we truly encountered unfailing love from a person. Human love waxes and wanes; it shuts down when it's hurt and withholds itself when it doesn't feel safe. As much as we may love another person or be loved by them, that love is imperfect.

Contrast this to the Lord's love for us. His love never wavers even when he is rejected. He gives all of himself every day when we are giving ourselves to other loves. He doesn't close off when we have pushed him away. He doesn't pursue another love when we are distracted. He always, infinitely, perfectly loves each of us. We need to let go of lesser things and open our hearts to that love today. Praise him for his love which is better than any other thing you could pursue.

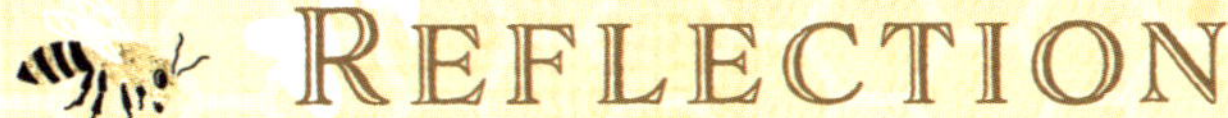

Reflection

How do you see God pursuing you even when you are seeking other things? What could cause you to grasp the depth of his love for you?

MY THOUGHTS

After reflecting on this devotion and follow-up questions, here are my thoughts.

MY RESPONSE

This is how I can apply the message to my life.

Through Jesus, therefore, let us continually offer to God a sacrifice of praise—the fruit of lips that openly profess his name.

HEBREWS 13:15 NIV

To me, this Scripture feels most like (check one)

☐ A PROMISE ☐ AN INSTRUCTION ☐ A TRUTH

Here's how it impacts me...

....

....

....

....

....

Prayer

GRATITUDE

I have been blessed with so many good things.
Here is what I am particularly thankful for this week.

REQUESTS

After reading and reflecting, here is what I'm asking God for.

WEEK 30

Called and Kept

I keep trying to reach the goal and get the prize for which God called me through Christ to the life above.

PHILIPPIANS 3:14 NCV

What is something that you know God has called you to that you have been struggling to fulfill? It could be a job, a friend to minister to, or even regular time in the Word. List out the reasons for your struggle. This may be more challenging than you anticipated because you don't feel equipped, you lack resources, or maybe you are worn out.

It is natural to come up against obstacles when we are fulfilling the Lord's calling in our lives, and we should even expect it! But if it is truly God who has called you to this particular thing, then you know that he has set your feet upon this path, and nothing can stop him from accomplishing it! It has less to do with your abilities and more with his faithfulness in you. Ask him to empower and embolden you to carry on with his calling in your life.

Reflection

God's calling on you does not depend on you to accomplish it. What does it look like for you to press on for the prize?

MY THOUGHTS

After reflecting on this devotion and follow-up questions, here are my thoughts.

MY RESPONSE

This is how I can apply the message to my life.

The one who calls you is faithful, and he will do it.

1 THESSALONIANS 5:24 NIV

To me, this Scripture feels most like (check one)

☐ A PROMISE ☐ AN INSTRUCTION ☐ A TRUTH

Here's how it impacts me...

PRAYER

GRATITUDE

I have been blessed with so many good things.
Here is what I am particularly thankful for this week.

REQUESTS

After reading and reflecting, here is what I'm asking God for.

WEEK 31

Treasure the Word

I have chosen the way of truth;
Your judgments I have laid before me.

PSALM 119:30 NKJV

In order to treasure God's Word, there are two things that the believer must do. First, remove things that have been given higher value than the Word. Second, put the Bible in the way. Identify the things in life that have been made more important than God's Word. These can be seen by the use of time: What things regularly have priority over time in the Word? Once these distractions have been identified, remove them. Treat anything that gets in the way of time spent building a relationship with Christ like an enemy.

Now it will be easier to accomplish the second step: put the Word in the way. Write Scripture verses on cards and put them in the car, on the fridge, in the bathroom. Keep the Bible close at hand. Reach for it first in the morning instead of looking at your phone. In order to learn to treasure the Word, it has to be treated as the most important thing in life.

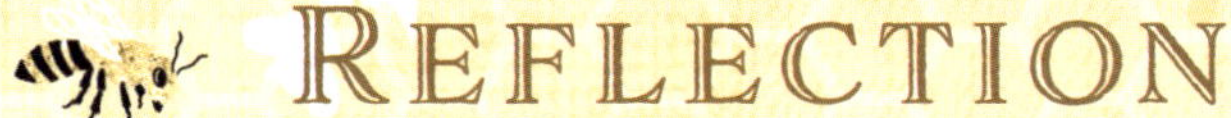

Reflection

Are there things you are treasuring over God's Word? How can you choose the way of truth instead?

MY THOUGHTS

After reflecting on this devotion and follow-up questions, here are my thoughts.

MY RESPONSE

This is how I can apply the message to my life.

"Those who follow the true way come to the light, and it shows that the things they do were done through God."

JOHN 3:21 NCV

To me, this Scripture feels most like (check one)

☐ A PROMISE ☐ AN INSTRUCTION ☐ A TRUTH

Here's how it impacts me...

PRAYER

GRATITUDE

I have been blessed with so many good things.
Here is what I am particularly thankful for this week.

REQUESTS

After reading and reflecting, here is what I'm asking God for.

WEEK 32

Practice

> This has been my practice:
> I obey your precepts.
>
> PSALM 119:56 NIV

We've surely all seen the effects of practice in our lives. Practice an instrument and there is success in the band competition. Practice a second language and we can speak it years later. Practice concepts from high school algebra, and years later it will still be there to use. But failure to practice means difficulty when it's time to try to pick it up again. "Use it or lose it," as they say.

This idea can apply to our relationships with Jesus too. Delighting ourselves in the Lord is not something that we will remember how to do if we have spent months filling our thoughts and spending our time on things other than him. Pursue the world and when we try to find our satisfaction in Christ again, we will struggle. But if we consistently practice, taking time every day to set our hearts and minds on Jesus, we will find a satisfied spirit dwelling within our souls.

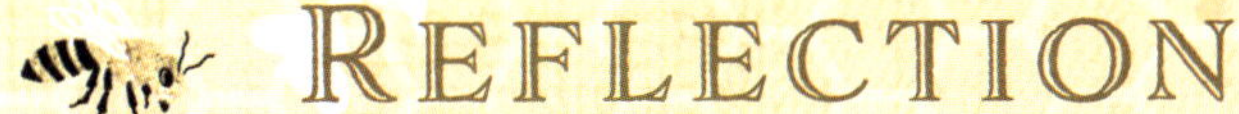

REFLECTION

How consistent are you in spending time in God's Word? Can you make time with God a priority?

MY THOUGHTS

After reflecting on this devotion and follow-up questions, here are my thoughts.

MY RESPONSE

This is how I can apply the message to my life.

Those who love your teachings will find true peace, and nothing will defeat them.

PSALM 119:165 NCV

To me, this Scripture feels most like (check one)

☐ A PROMISE ☐ AN INSTRUCTION ☐ A TRUTH

Here's how it impacts me…

Prayer

GRATITUDE

I have been blessed with so many good things.
Here is what I am particularly thankful for this week.

REQUESTS

After reading and reflecting, here is what I'm asking God for.

WEEK 33

Value

> Your teachings are worth more to me
> than thousands of pieces of gold and silver.
>
> PSALM 119:72 NCV

For most of us, speaking this psalm to the Lord truthfully and with conviction would probably cause us to be hesitant. It's a big statement, and if we look honestly at our lives, the verse will probably not reflect accurately.

Our pursuits show what we value if we take an honest look at life. For many of us, we would probably have to say that a version of the American Dream is governing our lives. We want maybe not the very best, but good things, nice things, easy living, and safety. We want financial security and provision. While these things are all worthy pursuits, if they are things we value most in life, we will find ourselves compromising the gospel in order to achieve stability.

Reflection

How do you keep God first in your life? What compromises can you see are getting in the way?

MY THOUGHTS

After reflecting on this devotion and follow-up questions, here are my thoughts.

MY RESPONSE

This is how I can apply the message to my life.

How much better
to get wisdom than gold,
to get insight
rather than silver!

PROVERBS 16:16 NIV

To me, this Scripture feels most like (check one)

☐ A PROMISE ☐ AN INSTRUCTION ☐ A TRUTH

Here's how it impacts me...

PRAYER

GRATITUDE

I have been blessed with so many good things.
Here is what I am particularly thankful for this week.

REQUESTS

After reading and reflecting, here is what I'm asking God for.

WEEK 34

Doubting Goodness

> Surely God is good to Israel,
> to those who are pure in heart.
>
> PSALM 73:1 NIV

Psalm 73 speaks of one of God's own who was thinking foolishly and did not understand why the Lord allowed certain good things to happen to the wicked while he himself suffered for living righteously. He became embittered toward God because of it. It was not until he entered God's sanctuary that he understood better. Even though he had been foolish and doubtful of God, he went on to speak about the mercy of God which would remain with him, counseling him, and giving him honor.

How often have we acted this same way? We see people walking in wickedness yet succeeding in life, at least in a worldly way, and we question the goodness and sovereignty of God. Do we forget that our God is a God of justice? Despite this, he continues to receive us back to him with open arms.

Reflection

Have you found yourself doubting God's goodness, sovereignty, and justice? He will deal kindly with you and help you trust him. All you have to do is ask!

MY THOUGHTS

After reflecting on this devotion and follow-up questions, here are my thoughts.

MY RESPONSE

This is how I can apply the message to my life.

*The Lord watches over
the path of the godly,
but the path of the wicked
leads to destruction.*

PSALM 1:6 NLT

To me, this Scripture feels most like (check one)

☐ A PROMISE ☐ AN INSTRUCTION ☐ A TRUTH

Here's how it impacts me...

PRAYER

GRATITUDE

I have been blessed with so many good things.
Here is what I am particularly thankful for this week.

REQUESTS

After reading and reflecting, here is what I'm asking God for.

WEEK 35

Favor

I sought Your favor with all my heart;
Be gracious to me according to Your word.

PSALM 119:58 NASB

Perhaps being popular isn't your thing, but you can probably admit to wanting to be found pleasing to others. Scripture says that Jesus, as a young man, grew in favor with God and people, so we know it's not a bad thing to be pleasing to others.

However, it is good practice to regularly ask yourself whose favor you are seeking. Are you seeking the approval of man, hoping to be admired and honored in your workplace, with family, or by friends? Are you spending your time doing things that you know will cause you to be seen in a good light so that you can fit in or be considered worthy of a certain group of people? Or can you genuinely say that you are pursuing the favor of the Lord with all your heart, looking to grow in righteousness and not concerning yourself with how the world views you? Once in a while, it is worthwhile to check the condition of the heart.

Reflection

When you look at your heart, can you honestly say that you are pursuing God's favor over the approval of others? How can you make this a reality?

MY THOUGHTS

After reflecting on this devotion and follow-up questions, here are my thoughts.

MY RESPONSE

This is how I can apply the message to my life.

Jesus increased in wisdom and stature and in favor with God and man.

LUKE 2:52 ESV

To me, this Scripture feels most like (check one)

☐ A PROMISE ☐ AN INSTRUCTION ☐ A TRUTH

Here's how it impacts me...

PRAYER

GRATITUDE

I have been blessed with so many good things.
Here is what I am particularly thankful for this week.

REQUESTS

After reading and reflecting, here is what I'm asking God for.

WEEK 36

Heart of Mercy

> You, O Lord, are a God merciful and gracious, slow to anger and abounding in steadfast love and faithfulness.
>
> PSALM 86:15 ESV

Riley was struggling with her roommate. Their habits, preferences, and values were growing markedly different. It took all of Riley's willpower to treat her roommate with basic respect. She knew that circumstances made it impossible to find a new roommate at the moment, but something had to change. She thought of how Jesus responded to people who mistrusted and mistreated him. He was humble, kind, and acted in truth regardless of their actions toward him.

Riley came to believe that God had given her an opportunity to love her roommate despite their differences, for as long as they were together. She prayed for God's compassion to fill her heart, that she would show mercy instead of condemnation, and have eyes to see her friend with unaffected love just as Jesus saw her. Perhaps there is someone in your life whom you need to see with the eyes of Jesus. Ask him to give you a heart of compassion for that person.

Reflection

Jesus looks at you with love and mercy even when you make mistakes. Is there someone in your life who needs you to show that same love? How can you begin to see them like Jesus does?

MY THOUGHTS

After reflecting on this devotion and follow-up questions, here are my thoughts.

MY RESPONSE

This is how I can apply the message to my life.

God can point to us in all future ages as examples of the incredible wealth of his grace and kindness toward us.

EPHESIANS 2:7 NLT

To me, this Scripture feels most like (check one)

☐ A PROMISE ☐ AN INSTRUCTION ☐ A TRUTH

Here's how it impacts me...

PRAYER

GRATITUDE

I have been blessed with so many good things.
Here is what I am particularly thankful for this week.

REQUESTS

After reading and reflecting, here is what I'm asking God for.

WEEK 37

Be Encouraged

> Confirm to your servant your promise,
> that you may be feared.
>
> PSALM 119:38 ESV

Sometimes we need a little reassurance of God's love for us. Life is hard, and it is easy to get discouraged when we are persevering in our challenging circumstances but don't feel the hand of God on our efforts. It's a simple truth that the Lord takes pleasure in confirming his love for us as well as the promises he has made. He loves encouraging us in our walk with him.

Our challenge today is to ask God to confirm again the things about which he has spoken: a promise from his Word, his calling on our lives. We may ask him for an encouraging word that will speak grace to our hearts. We can be specific in our requests, and therefore witness him proving himself faithful. Time and time again his saints have asked for a word, and time and time again he has spoken. Do it today and be encouraged to continue in your pursuit of God.

REFLECTION

Does your heart need encouragement from God? Ask him for it today. How does his faithfulness cause your faith to grow?

MY THOUGHTS

After reflecting on this devotion and follow-up questions, here are my thoughts.

MY RESPONSE

This is how I can apply the message to my life.

As high as the heavens
are above the earth,
so great is his faithful love
toward those who fear him.

PSALM 103:11 CSB

To me, this Scripture feels most like (check one)

☐ A PROMISE ☐ AN INSTRUCTION ☐ A TRUTH

Here's how it impacts me…

Prayer

GRATITUDE

I have been blessed with so many good things.
Here is what I am particularly thankful for this week.

REQUESTS

After reading and reflecting, here is what I'm asking God for.

WEEK 38

Hope against Hope

> Even when there was no reason for hope, Abraham kept hoping—believing that he would become the father of many nations. For God had said to him, "That's how many descendants you will have!"
>
> ROMANS 4:18 NLT

God has given us countless promises in his Word. The things about which he spoke to his people for generations still hold true for us today. They are the foundation of our hope which is based not in anything this world can offer but in the eternal nature of a faithful and good God. Our tendency is to forget all the reasons to hope when our earthly pleasures have disappointed us. But God mercifully reminds us that all is not lost according to his promises.

Pray this prayer adapted from Romans 4, placing your own name into the verses that speak of Abraham. May you remember that even when things look bleak in your life, God is still at work. He is able to accomplish what he has promised you. Hope against hope.

REFLECTION

Are you fully convinced that what God has promised, he will do? How can you set your hope in him and not waver in unbelief?

MY THOUGHTS

After reflecting on this devotion and follow-up questions, here are my thoughts.

MY RESPONSE

This is how I can apply the message to my life.

Take courage!
For I believe God.
It will be just as he said.

ACTS 27:25 NLT

To me, this Scripture feels most like (check one)

☐ A PROMISE ☐ AN INSTRUCTION ☐ A TRUTH

Here's how it impacts me…

....

....

....

....

....

PRAYER

GRATITUDE

I have been blessed with so many good things.
Here is what I am particularly thankful for this week.

REQUESTS

After reading and reflecting, here is what I'm asking God for.

WEEK 39

Lacking Nothing

> You open your hand;
> you satisfy the desire of every living thing.
>
> PSALM 145:16 ESV

Sophia was starting to realize that she tended to fill her time and thoughts with stuff. It was essentially a demonstration of her lack of faith in God to satisfy her desires. She bought new clothes, spent all her time with friends, and opened her social media apps anytime she had a spare moment. It all pointed to a disbelief in God's ability to be all she needed. She didn't trust that Jesus was more than enough, that she lacked nothing in him.

What does the way we spend our time and resources say about us? Does it demonstrate satisfaction in God and his care of us, or does it show that we don't trust him to be all we need? Today, let's watch how we spend time and what we fill our minds with. If we give ourselves time to thank God for his provision and care, does it change our mindsets? Spending time today acknowledging his goodness and faithfulness will remind us that he is our shepherd, and all we need.

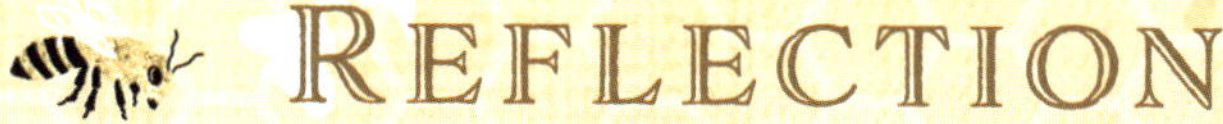

REFLECTION

What are your thoughts full of? Do you believe in the sufficiency of Christ? How can he satisfy your desires?

MY THOUGHTS

After reflecting on this devotion and follow-up questions, here are my thoughts.

MY RESPONSE

This is how I can apply the message to my life.

Give thanks to the Lord,
for he is good,
for his steadfast love
endures forever!

PSALM 107:1 ESV

To me, this Scripture feels most like (check one)

☐ A PROMISE ☐ AN INSTRUCTION ☐ A TRUTH

Here's how it impacts me...

Prayer

GRATITUDE

I have been blessed with so many good things.
Here is what I am particularly thankful for this week.

REQUESTS

After reading and reflecting, here is what I'm asking God for.

WEEK 40

Strangers on Earth

I am only a foreigner in the land.
Don't hide your commands from me!

PSALM 119:19 NLT

If you've ever lived in another country or in a culture different from your own, you understand how important it is to educate yourself in the proper way of living with people so different from yourself. Cultural blunders are real, and they can be embarrassing or even appalling. Studying the culture and the people you are living around helps you know how to interact in culturally acceptable ways.

As followers of Christ, we are not citizens of this world but of the kingdom of heaven. As such, the world is not our home, and we need to be informed on the proper way of living here with people who are different. Just as a cultural guide helps people living in another country, God's Word helps us understand how to live in a world that is not our true home. We can take time to ground ourselves in the instructions the Scriptures offer so that we are prepared to face all that we will encounter in this world.

REFLECTION

Do you think of this world as your final home? How can you live according to God's Word? How will you hold fast to his instructions?

MY THOUGHTS

After reflecting on this devotion and follow-up questions, here are my thoughts.

MY RESPONSE

This is how I can apply the message to my life.

With my whole heart
I have sought You;
Oh, let me not wander
from Your commandments!

PSALM 119:10 NKJV

To me, this Scripture feels most like (check one)

☐ A PROMISE ☐ AN INSTRUCTION ☐ A TRUTH

Here's how it impacts me…

....

....

....

....

....

PRAYER

GRATITUDE

I have been blessed with so many good things.
Here is what I am particularly thankful for this week.

REQUESTS

After reading and reflecting, here is what I'm asking God for.

WEEK 41

Embrace the Unknown

When I am afraid,
I will trust you.

PSALM 56:3 NCV

Sometimes it seems that God doesn't want us playing it safe in life. Many of us love our comfort, and we do our best to keep ourselves in calm waters close to the proverbial shoreline. We avoid things that cause pain. We stick to a well laid plan. But God isn't as interested in our safety and comfort as we are. He calls us into unknown situations, where the future is unclear, and we have to rely on him to be the lamp to our path. He changes our plans and leads us into circumstances that are sometimes painful but cause us to depend on him fully.

Be certain of this: that scary, unknown situation which God has led you into is so much safer than the calm, clearly marked road of your own choosing. Embrace the hard things that he has planned, knowing that they will bring goodness and reward if you follow him. He is worth trusting!

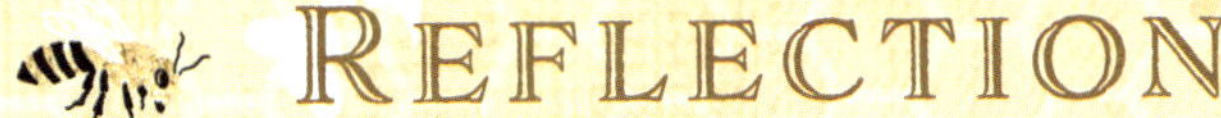

REFLECTION

What challenging situations are you facing right now? Can you see how they will bring you greater life? How can you give God glory through them?

MY THOUGHTS

After reflecting on this devotion and follow-up questions, here are my thoughts.

MY RESPONSE

This is how I can apply the message to my life.

I sought the Lord,
and He heard me,
and delivered me
from all my fears.

PSALM 34:4 NKJV

To me, this Scripture feels most like (check one)

☐ A PROMISE ☐ AN INSTRUCTION ☐ A TRUTH

Here's how it impacts me...

PRAYER

GRATITUDE

I have been blessed with so many good things.
Here is what I am particularly thankful for this week.

REQUESTS

After reading and reflecting, here is what I'm asking God for.

WEEK 42

Praiseworthy

> Fix your thoughts on what is true, and honorable, and right, and pure, and lovely, and admirable. Think about things that are excellent and worthy of praise.
>
> PHILIPPIANS 4:8 NLT

The news is a daily reminder of all that is wrong with the world. It's true that we are living in a time when lawlessness abounds, when God's instructions are ignored or mocked, and when the believer is made to feel like the enemy. But we need to remember that no matter what the current situation is in the world, we are always living in the midst of God's grace. Nothing in the world can change the fact that we have an inheritance in the age to come.

Let's set our minds on what is good, true, and worthy of giving God praise for his grace which sustains us. We are so grateful for his love which never grows tired, and the promise of eternity in glory with all the saints. We do not need to get bogged down with all that is wrong. We can turn our eyes to Jesus daily and remember to acknowledge all that is praiseworthy in him.

Reflection

Regardless of what is going on around you, you can be assured that your future is secure. How can you keep your focus on God and the promise of his glory?

MY THOUGHTS

After reflecting on this devotion and follow-up questions, here are my thoughts.

MY RESPONSE

This is how I can apply the message to my life.

The wisdom from above is first pure, then peace-loving, gentle, compliant, full of mercy and good fruits, unwavering, without pretense.

JAMES 3:17 CSB

To me, this Scripture feels most like (check one)

☐ A PROMISE ☐ AN INSTRUCTION ☐ A TRUTH

Here's how it impacts me...

....

....

....

....

....

PRAYER

GRATITUDE

I have been blessed with so many good things.
Here is what I am particularly thankful for this week.

REQUESTS

After reading and reflecting, here is what I'm asking God for.

WEEK 43

Counsel

> I will praise the LORD, who counsels me;
> even at night my heart instructs me.
>
> PSALM 16:7 NIV

We all know that our hearts are not the most reliable teachers. We are swayed by emotions and wrongful desires, and we're told by the world to follow our hearts which often leads us into sin. But God is the Creator of the heart, and he has good purposes for it too. In Psalms, David often speaks of his heart counseling or instructing him. The Lord speaks through our hearts by nudging our consciences and calling us back to righteousness when we are moving toward sin.

Through the Word and through our consciences, God instructs us in the right way to live. For that we praise him! Praise God that he does not abandon us to figure out life on our own or leave us walking in sin without reminding us of what is right and good. Praise God that he has given us his Word which is living and active and speaks to our spirits.

REFLECTION

How does God speak to your heart? What have you read in his Word lately that has counseled you?

MY THOUGHTS

After reflecting on this devotion and follow-up questions, here are my thoughts.

MY RESPONSE

This is how I can apply the message to my life.

You guide me
with your counsel,
and afterward
you will receive me
to glory.

PSALM 73:24 ESV

To me, this Scripture feels most like (check one)

☐ A PROMISE ☐ AN INSTRUCTION ☐ A TRUTH

Here's how it impacts me...

PRAYER

GRATITUDE

I have been blessed with so many good things.
Here is what I am particularly thankful for this week.

REQUESTS

After reading and reflecting, here is what I'm asking God for.

WEEK 44

Constant

> Do not cast me off in the time of old age;
> forsake me not when my strength is spent.
>
> PSALM 71:9 ESV

Perhaps you are young and capable; old age seems a lifetime away. Or perhaps you are now nearing your later years and feeling your body change. Regardless of your current age, there will come a time in life when you find yourself less capable than you once were. The strength of youth fades, perhaps taken prematurely by disease or injury. Our earthly bodies are perpetual reminders of the frailty of the human condition and of our dependence on a God who is not held back by human constraints.

There is beauty in knowing that our God's character is constant and will never change even as we do. He does not get weaker as time goes on. He is no less capable a hundred years from now than he is today. His faithfulness to guide, protect, and care for his children will never fail because he is unchanging. Praise him today for his constancy.

Reflection 

Do you sense your physical strength weakening? How does it bring you comfort to know that God is ever capable and unchanging in his ability to care for you?

MY THOUGHTS

After reflecting on this devotion and follow-up questions, here are my thoughts.

MY RESPONSE

This is how I can apply the message to my life.

I know whom I have believed and am persuaded that he is able to guard what has been entrusted to me until that day.

2 TIMOTHY 1 :12 CSB

To me, this Scripture feels most like (check one)

☐ A PROMISE ☐ AN INSTRUCTION ☐ A TRUTH

Here's how it impacts me...

Prayer

GRATITUDE

I have been blessed with so many good things. Here is what I am particularly thankful for this week.

REQUESTS

After reading and reflecting, here is what I'm asking God for.

WEEK 45

Road Closed

> I wait for the LORD, my soul waits,
> and in his word I hope.
>
> PSALM 130:5 ESV

Imagine you are on a road trip. You have an exciting destination in front of you, and you can't wait to get there. The trip should only be about twelve hours, but within an hour of starting, it is clear that this won't be a straightforward journey. Detours, traffic stops, and engine trouble cause delay after delay.

That's how life feels sometimes, right? What should be straightforward and easy turns out to be one delay or detour after another. When frustration starts to arise in our hearts, our capacity for patience depends on our ability to believe in God's purposes. He is at work creating something good for us in all the interruptions by taking us by the long way. Today, we can thank him for the delays in our days. We can thank him for changing our routes. We don't yet know what mercy is being shown to us on our journey.

REFLECTION

Do you find it hard to be patient and believe that God is in control when things aren't going as it seems they should? How can you trust in his goodness today?

MY THOUGHTS

After reflecting on this devotion and follow-up questions, here are my thoughts.

MY RESPONSE

This is how I can apply the message to my life.

The Lord is waiting
to show you mercy,
and is rising up
to show you compassion,
for the Lord is a just God.
All who wait patiently
for him are happy.

ISAIAH 30:18 CSB

To me, this Scripture feels most like (check one)

☐ A PROMISE ☐ AN INSTRUCTION ☐ A TRUTH

Here's how it impacts me...

Prayer

GRATITUDE

I have been blessed with so many good things.
Here is what I am particularly thankful for this week.

REQUESTS

After reading and reflecting, here is what I'm asking God for.

WEEK 46

Advocate

> You bless the righteous person, LORD,
> You surround him with favor as with a shield.
>
> PSALM 5:12 NASB

Consider the word *advocate* for a moment. An advocate is one who pleads another's cause. Jesus pleads in favor of us before the Father. He went to the full extent in advocating for us in order to remove God's divine wrath from his people and to have it directed toward himself instead. What amazing grace!

Think about how you can be an advocate for those in your life. Are you looking for opportunities to defend your brothers and sisters? Do you seek to surround them with favor, to plead their cause, to bless them? People are too often caught up in their own opinions and their own causes to defend those of someone else. Ask the Lord how you can honor and be an advocate for someone in need today.

Reflection

God defended you when you were in sin, going so far as to take the punishment that you deserved upon himself. How can you treat others that same way, blessing and honoring them instead of defending yourself?

MY THOUGHTS

After reflecting on this devotion and follow-up questions, here are my thoughts.

MY RESPONSE

This is how I can apply the message to my life.

The Lord God
is a sun and shield;
the Lord bestows
favor and honor.
No good thing
does he withhold
from those who
walk uprightly.

PSALM 84:11 ESV

To me, this Scripture feels most like (check one)

☐ A PROMISE ☐ AN INSTRUCTION ☐ A TRUTH

Here's how it impacts me...

PRAYER

GRATITUDE

I have been blessed with so many good things.
Here is what I am particularly thankful for this week.

REQUESTS

After reading and reflecting, here is what I'm asking God for.

WEEK 47

Ever-present Help

> God is our refuge and strength,
> an ever-present help in trouble.
> Therefore we will not fear,
> though the earth give way
> and the mountains fall into the heart of the sea.
>
> PSALM 46:1-2 NIV

God is an ever-present help in trouble. How comforting is that? We do not serve a God who stands aside and watches our pain. He interacts, he comes to our aid, he comforts and provides strength. We can pray this verse for ourselves today, entering in the things God is helping us through. We don't need to fear though our relationships are struggling, or though we wait in uncertainty about the future, or though we don't know how to share our faith with others, or though the pain of loss colors our days.

Whatever we face today, God is always with us. In all circumstances he is good. May this truth bring confidence in Christ and freedom to trust him implicitly. Stand in awe of his ability to control all things with perfect faithfulness.

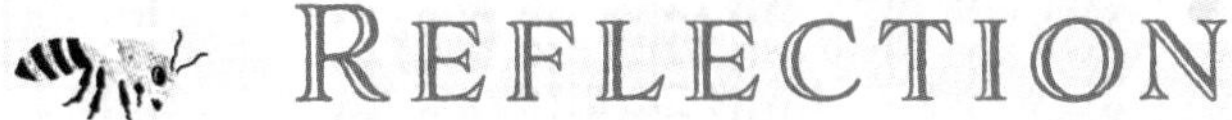

REFLECTION

What are you facing today that could cause fear if you let it? How can you trust in your ever-present help?

MY THOUGHTS

After reflecting on this devotion and follow-up questions, here are my thoughts.

MY RESPONSE

This is how I can apply the message to my life.

The Lord also will be a refuge for the oppressed,
A refuge in times of trouble.

PSALM 9:9 NKJV

To me, this Scripture feels most like (check one)

☐ A PROMISE ☐ AN INSTRUCTION ☐ A TRUTH

Here's how it impacts me...

Prayer

GRATITUDE

I have been blessed with so many good things.
Here is what I am particularly thankful for this week.

REQUESTS

After reading and reflecting, here is what I'm asking God for.

WEEK 48

Only Good in God

"You are my LORD;
I have no good apart from you."

PSALM 16:2 ESV

The faithfulness of the Lord is all around you. Throughout your day, may God show you all the small things he does so you are reminded of his steadfast and everlasting passion. May your intimacy with him grow powerfully as you walk by faith into his will for you. By that great love, you can walk without fear or hesitation and with great delight into the arms of a capable God.

May your obedience overcome the frailties of humanity. May you seek pleasure from no other sources. May you understand the supreme pleasure and joy of following Christ. May you rest securely in the knowledge that you are thoroughly and sincerely loved by God. May he be your goodness and light. Apart from him you have nothing at all.

REFLECTION

God is the source of all good and joy. You have been rescued by grace and kept by love. How can you use these truths to help you walk confidently in him?

MY THOUGHTS

After reflecting on this devotion and follow-up questions, here are my thoughts.

MY RESPONSE

This is how I can apply the message to my life.

Who do I have
in heaven but you?
And I desire nothing
on earth but you.

PSALM 73:25 CSB

To me, this Scripture feels most like (check one)

☐ A PROMISE ☐ AN INSTRUCTION ☐ A TRUTH

Here's how it impacts me…

Prayer

GRATITUDE

I have been blessed with so many good things.
Here is what I am particularly thankful for this week.

REQUESTS

After reading and reflecting, here is what I'm asking God for.

WEEK 49

Rich Decrees

> I have rejoiced in your laws
> as much as in riches.
>
> PSALM 119:14 NLT

The psalmist repeatedly speaks of God's Word as that which he delights in, trusts, treasures, and rejoices over. He studies it because he sees it as lifegiving. He finds comfort in it. He hurries to obey it. What dedication to God's Word! How does this compare to your own view of the Word? Do you see God's decrees as rich and something to be sought after? Is it something you long to study and meditate on because you understand the good that comes from that? Or does the Word feel more like a series of killjoy rules that prevent you from living as you would choose?

Our opinion of God's Word colors the entire way we live, and the wrong perspective will cause us to miss out on the blessings of obedience and of really knowing God. We need to ask ourselves today how we see the Word.

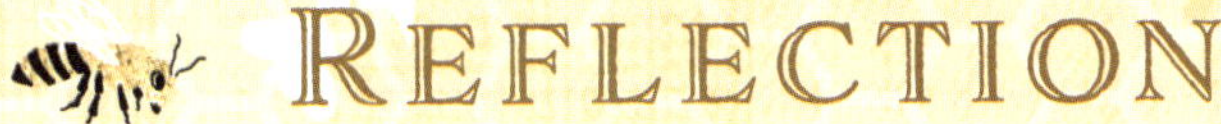

REFLECTION

Do you see God's Word as truth which you have fully dedicated yourself to pursuing? Or do you struggle to seek God in that way? How can you rejoice in his Word today?

MY THOUGHTS

After reflecting on this devotion and follow-up questions, here are my thoughts.

MY RESPONSE

This is how I can apply the message to my life.

Your words became to me
a joy and the delight
of my heart.

JEREMIAH 15:16 ESV

To me, this Scripture feels most like (check one)

☐ A PROMISE ☐ AN INSTRUCTION ☐ A TRUTH

Here's how it impacts me...

PRAYER

GRATITUDE

I have been blessed with so many good things.
Here is what I am particularly thankful for this week.

REQUESTS

After reading and reflecting, here is what I'm asking God for.

WEEK 50

Steadfast Love

> The steadfast love of the LORD never ceases;
> his mercies never come to an end;
> they are new every morning;
> great is your faithfulness.
>
> LAMENTATIONS 3:22-23 ESV

If you have had any amount of human interaction in your life, you understand the irregularity with which people love one another. You can be best friends at one moment, and worst enemies the next. You adore children, but sometimes they drive you crazy and you just want to be alone. Your coworker treats you with kindness one day, and the next you can't do anything right. Humanity is fickle, and our love is therefore capricious.

Imagine if God loved us the same way. If his love were based on our ability to love with consistency, we'd be sunk. Instead, his love is steadfast, unwavering, and not at all dependent on our propensity to do things right. We can thank him for that love today and ask him to empower us to demonstrate that same love to those in our lives.

REFLECTION

Aren't you thankful that God's faithfulness is not dependent on you? His persistent love never changes despite your inconsistencies. How does his love empower you to love others?

MY THOUGHTS

After reflecting on this devotion and follow-up questions, here are my thoughts.

MY RESPONSE

This is how I can apply the message to my life.

Has his faithful love
ceased forever?
Is his promise at an end
for all generations?

PSALM 77:8 CSB

To me, this Scripture feels most like (check one)

☐ A PROMISE ☐ AN INSTRUCTION ☐ A TRUTH

Here's how it impacts me...

....

....

....

....

....

Prayer

GRATITUDE

I have been blessed with so many good things.
Here is what I am particularly thankful for this week.

REQUESTS

After reading and reflecting, here is what I'm asking God for.

WEEK 51

Abounding Grace

God is able to make all grace overflow to you,
so that, always having all sufficiency in everything,
you may have an abundance for every good deed.

2 CORINTHIANS 9:8 NASB

You are abounding in grace. Never does God leave you in want. You have all that you need available to you for all time. What a gift! What needs do you have today? Ask the Lord for his overflowing grace to prove all-sufficient in your life. Are you feeling heavy, overwhelmed, or anxious? Ask the Lord to sustain you for every good work which he has planned for you.

The incredible thing about our God is that he does not stand around watching us struggle; he is near to the brokenhearted, he makes grace abound when we need it, he strengthens us, he gives all we need. Accept that truth for yourself today and take your stand in it.

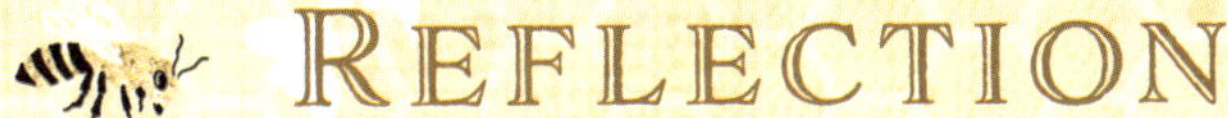

Reflection

Thank God that you don't have to earn his grace and that it stays with you everywhere you go every day that you live. How have you seen his abounding grace in your life?

MY THOUGHTS

After reflecting on this devotion and follow-up questions, here are my thoughts.

MY RESPONSE

This is how I can apply the message to my life.

What you are experiencing is truly part of God's grace for you. Stand firm in this grace.

1 PETER 5:12 NLT

To me, this Scripture feels most like (check one)

☐ A PROMISE ☐ AN INSTRUCTION ☐ A TRUTH

Here's how it impacts me...

PRAYER

GRATITUDE

I have been blessed with so many good things.
Here is what I am particularly thankful for this week.

REQUESTS

After reading and reflecting, here is what I'm asking God for.

WEEK 52

Desire to Learn

> You made me and formed me with your hands.
> Give me understanding so I can learn your commands.
>
> PSALM 119:73 NCV

The ability to learn and pursue knowledge are gifts from God. His creation is astounding, and we were made to discover it! But what does the Bible tell us about learning? The psalmist asks for understanding not so he could pursue the things that sparked his interest, but so that he can learn the commands of God.

While our passions are certainly gifts, it is always important to come back to the foundational reason the Lord gave us the ability to learn. He is a God that we can know. He is discoverable. His Word holds promises, revelations, ideas that no person could come up with. Scripture is full of good commands that we can discover. We need to make sure that our passions do not cloud out the joy of pursuing understanding of the Word.

REFLECTION

You have been given a mind to explore, discover, and learn about God's creation, and about God himself. What things are you passionate about? What drives your desire to learn or grow your understanding?

MY THOUGHTS

After reflecting on this devotion and follow-up questions, here are my thoughts.

MY RESPONSE

This is how I can apply the message to my life.

It is the spirit in a person—
the breath from the Almighty—
that gives anyone
understanding.

JOB 32:8 CSB

To me, this Scripture feels most like (check one)

☐ A PROMISE ☐ AN INSTRUCTION ☐ A TRUTH

Here's how it impacts me...

Prayer

GRATITUDE

I have been blessed with so many good things.
Here is what I am particularly thankful for this week.

REQUESTS

After reading and reflecting, here is what I'm asking God for.

Prayer Requests

	DATE	WHAT I AM BELIEVING FOR	HOW AND WHEN GOD ANSWERED

Prayer Requests

	DATE	WHAT I AM BELIEVING FOR	HOW AND WHEN GOD ANSWERED

Prayer Requests

	DATE	WHAT I AM BELIEVING FOR	HOW AND WHEN GOD ANSWERED

Prayer Requests

	DATE	WHAT I AM BELIEVING FOR	HOW AND WHEN GOD ANSWERED

Prayer Requests

	DATE	WHAT I AM BELIEVING FOR	HOW AND WHEN GOD ANSWERED

Prayer Requests

	DATE	WHAT I AM BELIEVING FOR	HOW AND WHEN GOD ANSWERED

Prayer Requests

	DATE	WHAT I AM BELIEVING FOR	HOW AND WHEN GOD ANSWERED

Prayer Requests

	DATE	WHAT I AM BELIEVING FOR	HOW AND WHEN GOD ANSWERED

Prayer Requests

	DATE	WHAT I AM BELIEVING FOR	HOW AND WHEN GOD ANSWERED

Prayer Requests

	DATE	WHAT I AM BELIEVING FOR	HOW AND WHEN GOD ANSWERED

Prayer Requests

	DATE	WHAT I AM BELIEVING FOR	HOW AND WHEN GOD ANSWERED